# DANCING WITH DEATH

# THE BATTLE OF A SUICIDAL MIND

## Dawna A. Wright

Dancing With Death: The Battle of a Suicidal Mind

ISBN-13: 978-0-692-94533-9

# Dedication

To the woman who birthed me and did all she could to make sure I was successful in everything I did, my mother, thank you for making sure I was rooted in Christ and able to progress through life's challenges. You are so strong and resilient. I get that from you! You were able to bounce back from everything life sent your way and I'm happy to be your daughter. You're an amazing mother, friend, business woman, aunt, sister, grandmother, and wife. May God forever show you favor and abundant blessings. I love you.

To every family, community, church, and individual who has ever had to experience the loss of a loved one due to suicide, I write this for you. For anyone facing challenges and struggling with whether or not life is an option, this book is for you. Stay strong! Fight through it! What God has for you outweighs whatever the enemy (Satan) is causing you to believe is prevalent. You are more than conquerors. You are not who people say you are. You are who God says you are. Be at peace and know that ALL things work together for your good. May this book bless you and give you peace in Jesus precious name.

Amen!

# ~Table of Contents~

# Acknowledgements

**Special Thanks**:

To my Lord and Savior, Jesus Christ! I don't deserve the favor on my life but you see fit to use this nobody to share with everybody what you've done. My only work, here on earth, is to do your will. I walk in it. I receive it. I believe it!

To my Bishop, Henry Fernandez, you have the heart of God. You carry the weight of pastoring thousands of hurting people and you do so with grace and wisdom. You are a light that shines bright in a dark world. I love that you are transparent, down to earth, and caring. I serve under the greatest leader I've ever known. Your faith will continue to spread like wild fire through-out the Faith Center and surrounding nations. You are loved and appreciated and it's my prayer that you walk in everything God has for you.

To the Harrison's (Deon and Raymond), thank you for never abandoning me. You guys have remained by my side through thick and thin, since my childhood. I can always count on you both to cover me in prayer and speak life into me. Deon, we share more than a birthday, but an unconditional love that knows no bounds. I will forever be grateful for our connection.

To Juliet, my friend, thank you for praying with and for me. You are the first person ever to cry for the hurtful things I experienced. I will never forget your diligence in helping me to understand and work through my challenges. You are the perfect example of unconditional commitment and love.

To Pastor Inger Hanna, you are one of the most authentic pastors I have ever met! Your love for people amazes me. Thank you for always having my back! Thank you for pouring into me and allowing me into your home. Thank you for never judging me but accepting me for who I am while pushing me into my purpose. Your laugh is contagious and your sense of humor is healing to the soul.

To Minister Darlene, you are breathtaking. Your grace is contagious. Thank you for dealing with me in grace. Thank you for pouring into me and praying for me. Thank you for helping me transform into a beautiful woman of God. Your poise perpetuates purpose. Your smile and laugh brings hope. Thank you for allowing me to participate in your mentorship program and helping me better prepare for ministry, marriage, and the marketplace. You are a blessing and God has a great work for you! You are called to nations!

To Divine Connection (Marquia, Kerry-Ann, and Sharifa), I love you guys like my sisters. Thank you all for being the close group of friends that I can depend on for anything! Marquia, you fight for and with me in the battle trenches and will forever be a part of my life. You're my best friend. Kerry (my other bestie), you are graceful and God has connected us for great reason. You're the big sister I have always wanted and I cannot imagine a life that doesn't include you. Sharifa, your strength is unbelievable. I'm so glad to call you friend. You have a fire that can refine any situation. Our group will change nations. Thank you all for accepting me and loving on me in the good and bad times.  You are my sisters and you guys make life more manageable. I love you all!

To Joanna, whew! I thank God for sending you into my life. You keep me humble and you exemplify the meaning of what it means to love unconditionally. You are thoughtful and walk in a GRACE that rubs off on me. You push me past my limits and make sure I am able to ride out this race called life. Thank you for taking the time to pour into me and listen to me whenever I need it. I love you so much!

To Minister Thomas Glass, thank you for making sure I continued to come to church. I would never have written this book if it wasn't for your persistence and patience. Thank you for being the positive male role model I needed in my life. You are an angel in disguise.

To Minister Philbert Lake, you changed my views of how a leader should be. You are led by the Holy Spirit; the nuggets you pour into the music ministry as well as members at the Faith Center, exudes in the worship and personal lives of everyone under your leadership. Thank you for knowing my name and being obedient to the calling on your life.

To Minister Lenzetta Lake, thank you for your transparency and openness. You helped me realize that I was not alone in my experiences and that God can use any and everything to make his will evident in my life. It's your relationship that allowed me to survive numerous suicide attempts on my life. Thank you for loving on me. Thank you for being my sister in times of need.

To Frankia, you are beautiful on the inside and out. Thank you for your thoughtfulness and patience. Thank you for the kind words spoken into and over my life. Thank you for praying with me and believing in me. People like you needed to be planted in every church.

To Mrs. Toby, you fight for me in ways that I don't even know how to fight for myself. You are thoughtful, giving, and humble. I love that you are who you are, regardless of what's happening around you. I'm so glad to be connected to you. You changed my views on what a mentor is and I appreciate you so much. I know that you will always have my back! Thank you for helping me grow gracefully.

Janice Johnson: Thank you for every bowl of Chicken Souse that I have ever eaten! Your cooking brings pure joy. Your hugs help heal my heart. Your smile You are graceful in everything you do. You see me at my best and my worst. Thank you for taking on one of the most difficult roles in my life. I love you.

To Harriet Bastian (The Faithful Usher), you were the FIRST person I came in contact with at the Faith Center. I was so lost and scared, but your hospitality and kindness planted a seed that helped me blossom into who and where I am today. I came into the Faith Center wondering how this huge church could help me want to live again. You had no idea who I was or what I was going through, but you never left my side and remained on your post. I will forever remember your name and your kindness.

To Natasha Watkins: you embody the meaning of FRIEND and SISTER. I can't think of one word that captures the true essence of what you have been in my life. You are a minister to so many but I'm just glad to call you friend and sister. You are loyal, patient, selfless, and pure of heart. Thank you for praying with and for me. Friends like you come once in a lifetime, but God saw fit to connect you to me. You will change the hearts of nations! Beautifully created! I love you sis.

# Endorsements

Dawna Wright is a woman with many layers: Someone that is extraordinarily gifted, but has also been deeply conflicted; exceptionally intelligent, but has endured mental torment; highly competitive, yet has wanted to quit life. Through it all, each layer reveals a woman, who at her core, loves God.

Dawna has a passion to serve and a compassion for the hurting and I liken her to a modern day Mary Magdalene...A women who Jesus delivered from tormenting spirits and she became His faithful follower and devoted servant. She was the FIRST one Jesus appeared to after His resurrection! Just as Mary Magdalene was chosen to carry the message of LIFE to those who mourn and wept, I believe Dawna has also been chosen to proclaim "He's Alive and because He lives we can face tomorrow."

This book is a symbol of her will to live and to help others live, it is a part of her testimony and her triumph.

Inger Hanna
Theos' Family Church & Enrichment Center
Elder/Pastor

# CHAPTER 1

## *The Dance, My Life*

{Romans 8:28, NLT}

"And we know that God causes everything to work together for the good of those who love God and are called according to his purpose for them."

Dawna, the light that breaks all darkness (the meaning of her name). Yet darkness hovered around her like death around rotting flesh. Her very name was subjected to the attack of darkness (Satan). Any bit of light that tried to flicker in her life would constantly be concealed by grim disheartening circumstances. Before she could even properly utter her first words she had already experienced a myriad of hurt, rejection, and disappointment.

Her early years of life consisted of repeated physical abuse and witnessing her mother beaten senseless by her father. Her memories consisted of constant yelling, hiding under beds, fear of people, sexual abuse, alcoholism, molestation, neglect, and emotional abuse. The people she should have been able to lean on and trust were the very same people that pulled the rug from beneath her fragile legs. Dawna learned at a young age never to trust anyone. To trust was a sign of weakness and risked exposing eerie family secrets and hidden agendas. So many secrets! So many lies and deception! In public, things were one way but behind closed doors it was a completely different story.

Dawna grew up in a family of God-fearing church folk. She attended choir practice, bible study, evening services, and prayer services on a regular basis. The church motto was, "If it made you grin it was sin." Her family made up a large portion of the church and were pretty well-respected in the church and community. Her life revolved around the church, not God. Church was more about following rules and church bylaws than building a sound relationship with God. No wearing of pants! No clapping in service (was seen as

7

praising people instead of God)! No jewelry! No make-up! No work or basketball games on the Sabbath.

Did I mention that Dawna was also a star athlete basketball player? Her ball handling skills and jump shot was something to be contended with. She was a smart kid, but had so many behavioral problems. She despised authority and was known for being a tomboy and bully. She was kicked out of numerous schools for fighting staff and students. Her very presence demanded attention wherever she went. She was always the center of attention (mostly negative). If people only knew the real reasons behind her behavior and misdirected aggression, they would have treated her so differently.

There was a time in Dawna's young life where she created a world of lies and fantasies in hopes of experiencing genuine love and security. She said whatever she needed to say in order to get the responses she was in search of (sympathy, empathy, love, and security). With years of counseling and psychotherapy she discovered that her creation of this fraudulent world was done as a survival mechanism to help meet her basic needs of love and protection. She would make up stories about being grabbed off the street while walking and then raped. For years, she told people about being raped by strangers and its negative impact on her life, while in reality she was being molested by her grandfather and stepfathers. When she told the truth about what was really happening to her, she was said to be a liar and simply confused. Dawna began to wonder if she really experienced the things that haunted her at night. She remembers that pain, even now, of being let down by the people that should have protected her. Amongst the lies she conjured up were painful realities of what she had to endure on a continual basis. She would tell people the hurt she was experiencing and they would gossip, make fun of her, and call her crazy or delusional. How could a young girl trust herself or those entrusted to protect her when her experience reminded her that whatever she had to say didn't matter? She felt so alone and trapped. She woke up every morning with either someone's fingers inside of her or having to lay on top of a man in order to please his sexual desires. She vividly remembers her stepfather lifting her up and wrapping her legs around his waist while pressing his genitals against hers. Initially, it was awkward and uncomfortable but, with time, she came to enjoy the feeling of her step father's genital pressed against hers, which caused her to feel even guiltier about what was happening. Her body responded to what was happening but her mind was tormented and confused. Was he wrong or was he right because of how her body responded to what he was doing? Was this even abuse or was it just solicited perversion?

So many people have similar experiences, but remain silent in hopes that things will work themselves out or maybe it's not a big deal. The mistrust for people (especially in her family) was the root of her feelings of rejection, disconnect, hopelessness, and pain. It seemed as though every person that came into her life took something from her, whether it be her dignity, innocence, sense of safety, well-being, trust, or sense of self. In order for her to receive the love she needed, she had to give up something or create a situation that demanded the attention she very much longed for. The price she had to pay to receive love was costly and how she received that love made no difference to her. Dawna learned quickly that she didn't deserve unconditional love and that, in reality, no relationship ever lasted. If she wanted "real" love, she would have to pay for it with her actions.

This little girl came from a dysfunctional family where bad things happened a lot but remained protected by secrets and continued denial. She was taught to protect the well-being of the family ahead of herself. It was better to suffer in silence than to openly embarrass the family. Maybe her childhood was filled with some good memories but they were few and far between. What she did remember was: hiding under beds, being beaten senseless, sexual abuse, shame, incest, bed-wetting, nightmares, incarceration, deceit, confusion, fighting, verbal abuse, violence, death, manipulation, pornography, and perversion (most, before the age of 17).

Her behavior eventually started to spiral out of control due to the lack of control in her personal life. Consequently, she was locked in padded rooms, admitted to mental hospitals, kicked out of schools, detained in juvenile detention center, sent away to boarding school, and written off as "crazy", unmanageable, and unworthy to be loved and accepted. Her acting out came with negative attention, but attention none the less. She craved love, acceptance, and attention; and that need for attention soon became the basis for most of her rebellious behavior and fascination with dying.

With each experience and situation, people started to slowly give up on her then she eventually gave up on herself. Dawna's first thoughts of suicide came about in elementary school and her first attempt was made in middle school. Each negative experience became a part of who she was. Each memory plagued her. Every bad touch, every hurtful word that was said, and every unheard cry for help contributed to her feelings of hopelessness and obsession with dying. If the only way she could receive love was to give away parts of herself that she didn't want to, then life wasn't worth living. In her mind, giving her love to the wrong people for the right reasons was worth the temporary love and acceptance she so longed for. But the pain it caused was almost unbearable.

Almost every relationship and connection outside of her home exemplified some residue of what she was experiencing in her home. Most of her relationships were filled with perversion, deception, and rejection. Her relationship with the church enforced the following: Don't trust people (especially in the church), protect others for the betterment of the greater good, bad people are in church too, and that if you are a bad child, no one will ever believe you. The church also taught her that God won't love her unless she was able to follow all His (God) rules. So there she was, a confused young lady, bruised, battered, ashamed, and hopeless, feeling as though not even God was on her side. What good was she to anyone? She was a walking target where any and every one could take their turn getting what they

needed from her as if she were a used paper towel (crushed, dampened, and stained).

She believed that her only hope to be heard would occur at church, but church was like a movie where everyone came playing a specific role to see who would receive the award for best actor. No doubt her family had won several Emmys for best actors. People were living all sorts of lies, but attended church pretending to be something else. The only reason she even went to church was because she didn't want to go to hell. She had heard about hell and feared the feeling of hot fire melting her skin and bones. An eternity of torture just didn't seem worth missing church for. The idea of having a relationship with God didn't seem within her reach, yet she always felt as though God had her back, despite all the craziness that went on her life. Most of the time she attended church, she would pretend like everything was fine, hoping someone would give her a hug and simply ask, "Are you okay?" Dawna would look forward to ANY type of affection she could receive, whether it be a hug, a smile, or maybe even a soft touch. After all, didn't God create her to be loved? She longed for affection so much that she would allow different boys, men, and women to sleep with her in hopes of feeling something comforting. She would imagine a certain type of love and affection in her head that filled her needs, but once the act actually happened she just ended up feeling ashamed, used, devalued, and worse off than she started.

She just wanted to be heard. No one really gave her the time of day because of her reputation for being a liar, attention-seeker, and trouble maker. If only people knew what her stepfathers and other family members were doing behind closed doors or what her grandfather did every morning. Her experience was muzzled by the secrecy of her family. She couldn't see a light at the end of her tunnel and she continued to feel that way, even as an adult.

She remembered feeling so overwhelmed one day and reaching out to someone in the church to help her process those feelings. She spilled out everything on her heart and that person told other people what was said and then made jokes about it. Those people then talked about her to other people and she was eventually labeled "the troubled girl" who lies. She felt so alone and helpless. She eventually started to struggle with isolation and the thoughts of suicide continued to rare its ugly head. She experimented with different ways of hurting herself (mostly, self-inflicted injuries) but none quite quenched her need for relief. None of her attempts were obviously successful. But the physical and emotional scars left behind were evident.

Those suicidal thoughts plagued her mind until her early 30's. Attempt after attempt; reaching out constantly; hoping that someone would hear her cry for help and for ONCE, answer. Whether by Facebook Posts or Text Messages or even letters; she fought to be heard but people could not see her hurt and she honestly believed that no one wanted to deal with what she was carrying. She was stuck in a cycle of feeling as though she had no way out. She couldn't move forward nor could she go backwards. Death appeared to be her only option! So she found herself gaining comfort from envisioning her death over and over again.

Suicide doesn't just pertain to a physical death. There can be emotional and spiritual suicide where emotions are completely shut off, a separation from the covering of church family occurs, or a deliberate disconnect from God. To experience each form of suicide simultaneously is dangerous and has detrimental consequences. When emotionally cut off without any support, the risk for committing physical suicide is greatly increased.

It makes sense that in going through trials and challenges, we look to connect and communicate with other people. God created us to connect with others. We are social beings, wonderfully and fearfully made. Unfortunately, that young lady (which was me) was made to believe that opening up and wanting to connect with others was simply unacceptable, unreasonable, and unattainable.

### ~Relationship with Family~

When I imagine family I picture hugs, soft whispers, holding of hands, encouraging words, unconditional love, and the smell of turkey bacon at noon. I imagine a family that speaks positive words into and over my life. Not every family is perfect, but a family centered on love,

I believed, could move mountains. I wanted that so badly. I use to find comfort in imagining being curled up in the arms of a family member and experiencing genuine connection. There were no consistent healthy existing relationships between my family and me. I, at one point, did have some family members where I was able to visit their homes, eat lunch, and just chill without worrying about anything. But, for the most part, I didn't feel like I could really open up to anyone about what was really going on in my life.

As a child, I felt like the church was only made to help adults because they were the ones who were always right, even when they did wrong. Reaching out to the community meant that I would be shamed, let-down, and ridiculed. I learned at an early age never to depend on anyone. To expect anything from anyone was opening myself up to experiencing disappointment, mistreatment, and rejection. I tried to have friends, but that never quite worked out for me. I just never really fit in. I felt like the only way for me to get people to love and accept me was by lying and presenting myself as a victim. I felt as though I was too needy, mean, and different ("weird") to be accepted amongst my family or peers. Most of those beliefs and experiences carried over into adulthood and affected most, if not all my relationships. It's as if I was stuck in time, never having healed as a child. That unhealed hurt unraveled in every area of my life and the thoughts of suicide continued to seduce my spirit and soul.

I remember getting into an argument with my mother one time at church. I got so upset that I went outside, in the pouring rain, and sat on the wall with my hands folded just so that I could embarrass my mother. I wasn't thinking about how "disturbed" or rebellious I looked. My only concern was "paying my mother back." How twisted does your thinking have to be if you feel as though the best way to hurt someone else is by hurting yourself? Unfortunately, that would remain my reason for wanting to die for a long time. I wanted payback! That's a lot of built up pain if you're willing to hurt yourself to make a point. Situations like this fed my obsession with dying because I figured that my voice was much louder in my death than it could ever be in life.

My obsession with suicide was rooted in rejection. I was living to avoid rejection! One unhealthy relationship after another, I spiraled out of control. I was on a journey that consisted of me: crying out for help, feeling trapped, walking out of purpose, and not experiencing the real joy God had instore for me. The following chapters address these experiences and how I was able to eventually overcome my dance with death.

Although my story started out tragic and painful, God used every petrifying detail and turned it around for my good. For every experience that should have killed me, it gave me new life. It took me a while to realize my value, but when God allowed me to see myself through His eyes, I began to walk in a newness. I have been walking in that newness ever since. God can and will show you who you are. Allow Him to have His way in your life. Ask Him to use your details to develop you.

At the conclusion of each chapter there are three interactive activities to be completed. These activities can be completed individually or with a group. I would suggest having someone available to share your experiences with, as some of the topics can be sensitive and thought-provoking. Although it is recommended that you complete some of the activities with someone else, they can also be completed individually.

**Chapter Activity**: These are a series of questions that encourage you to identify, reflect, and share certain experiences and revelations from your life. Some of the activities can be challenging, but complete them to the best of your ability. Take your time when answering the questions. If you can, find a quiet place to complete the activities.

**Self-Reflection**: This section allows for written journal entries of your feelings, concerns, ideas, and experiences. Answering some of the questions in the "chapter activity" might give you the urge to express your feelings. Therefore, use this section to write down whatever it is your feeling or feel the need to say.

**Picture It**: "Picture It" focuses on allowing the opportunity for visual expression of your thoughts, feelings, and ideas. It is sometimes easier to draw when expressing deep feelings. Use this section to draw whatever comes to mind after completing the chapter readings.

# The Dance, My Life: Activity

What are some incidents you recall from childhood that possibly affect your present day response, reactions, and tolerance to life situations?

What are some things you find yourself struggling with in life?

Do you deal with stressors in a healthy manner? Explain…

Have you ever had negative consequences from the way you've dealt with situations in your life? Explain…

# ~SELF- REFLECTION~

# <u>PICTURE IT</u>

# CHAPTER 2

## *To Live or Not to Live*

{John 10:10, AMP}

"The thief comes only in order to steal and kill and destroy. I came that they may have and enjoy life, and have it in abundance [to the full, till it overflows]."

I wanted to live, but between the hurt and isolation I was experiencing, that dance with death seemed all the more appealing. I felt like I was always walking around with a chip on my shoulder, feeling rejected and hurt about everything! I had become so sensitive to criticism and redirection. I felt like I always had something to prove. I could never do or say enough to be what others needed me to be. Failing wasn't an option for me. Yet, I felt like a failure at almost everything I did. The only area of my life I felt I had control in was whether or not I would live.

I imagined how my funeral would be and how my death could finally stop the battle in my mind, not really thinking about all the other consequences. I imagined thousands of people at my funeral, talking about how good of a person I was and the tragedy of my death. I was comforted by the thoughts of others speaking kind words about me and crying for me, seeing as though no one had ever cried for me when I was alive. The thousands of "RIP" comments on my social media brought me a displaced peace. I believed that what I couldn't obtain in life, I would obtain in death! I knew that people would be forced to pay attention. People would have to listen. I had to get my moment of acknowledgement, even if it cost me my life. This skewed way of thinking was all the hope I believed I had, but wait until you see how God shifted my thought process and gave me a renewed mind.

There was a battle happening in my mind. The battle was between my hunger for life and fascination with death. The enemy (Satan) wanted me to believe that I had nothing to live for, while God reassured me I had everything to live for. I battled with understanding why I had to emotionally pay for what others physically did to me. Why was I more prone to feelings of depression? Why did I feel so alone? I just wanted my mind to stop racing. I wanted to feel excited about something and experience real joy for once in my life. You know? The joy that didn't disappear after a few days or weeks. I wanted to sleep without having nightmares. I wanted to be special to someone, anyone! I wanted to have friends and family that appreciated me and loved me.

Although I had a strong root in rejection, I was also firmly rooted in Christ. So even when I wanted to take myself out, God wasn't having it! My relationship with Jesus was kind of like my personal "cheat code." For every stage of life I entered, God found a way to get through to me despite me trying to escape this world. God's persistence is what kept me alive. I know it sounds a bit cliché, but how else can you explain numerous suicide attempts without any success? How do you explain my ability to graduate from college and still have a sound mind? Luck? I don't think there is enough luck in this world to bring me through the mess I was in! And I have a feeling that you can probably say the same thing. My connection with God was all I really had. I'd talk to Him because I felt a connection with Him that I didn't quite feel with anyone else. Does that sound weird? Maybe I'm being too spiritual? It was so real for me. It felt real. Countless nights, I would pray for God to take me out of my misery and kill me before I did something I could never take back. Nightmares replayed in my head over and over again. Constant ridicule! So many mistakes. No love! No patience. It didn't seem fair. If this is what life had to offer I didn't want it! If choosing God meant I had to endure this much pain, I didn't want Him either or at least so I thought. But God still had my back in the midst of my confusion and discontent. Life didn't seem real plausible for me but I lived.

What exactly did choosing to live mean? For me, that meant facing what felt was unbearable hurt, connecting with people, accepting things and people I couldn't change, remembering the memories I buried, confessing hurt, facing weaknesses, standing up to challenges, and accepting responsibility for the things I had a part in creating.

In my mind, choosing not to live meant that there would be an immediate halt to my bad experiences. But deep down I knew that was just a mask covering up the real issues I was facing. I knew I was somehow being deceived but I didn't know how to fight back! See, scripture says that Satan is like a roaring lion, looking for who he can devour (1 Peter 5:8). The attack almost always starts in the mind. What you think manifests in your feelings and what you feel becomes action. The enemy will make a suggestion (in our minds) and we then take that suggestion and create chaos. In choosing not to live, I just hoped the chaos I chose to receive would stop!

I was absolutely convinced that I could obtain more in death than I ever could in life. I 100% believed that death was my only answer!

## ~The Mind Games~

In my mind, the entire world was against me! Everyone was fake and had ill-intentions. At different times, I felt as though even God didn't have my best interest at heart. I felt as though God viewed me like everyone else did and there was no way He could love me unconditionally. I was alone and no bible verse, worship song, altar call, prayer, person, or drug could help me feel any different. I felt as though I made God so angry from my previous mistakes that He wanted nothing to do with me. I felt as though God saying He cared about me was a very bad joke at my expense. One minute I thought He loved me and the next I knew He hated me. The back and forth in my mind was almost unbearable. The instability made me feel as though I could never be "normal" or recuperate from my decisions. I would forever be viewed as inconsistent and of no value. I didn't stand a chance, even if I wanted to recover, because I would forever be stuck in the prison I created in my mind. I was, emotionally, serving a life sentence.

The relationship I believed I had with God was as inconsistent as the thoughts in my head. I recognized that whatever happens in reality first starts in the mind. I was often told that whatever you think becomes what you do and what you do becomes who you are. Well, in my mind I was a hopeless young lady that didn't stand a chance in this big world. I had forgotten that "Greater is He that is in me than he that is in the world" (1 John 4:4). What that meant was that the God in me was much bigger than the enemy (Satan) who was in the world. If I could just believe that in my mind and heart then just maybe I could become what I thought. I needed my body to come in alignment with my mind and my mind to be in alignment with God's Word and Will for my life.

I had to make up in my mind (FIRST) that death was not the solution to my problems. Death only removed the opportunity of me ever getting the chance to respond to my problems. To live or not live was indeed a decision I had to make. Would my need for attention always outweigh my will to live? This question plagued me for years.

What thought, idea, or situation is making you feel as though your life has no value? What's holding you back from walking in your full purpose? What thoughts are holding you captive right this moment? Take a minute to write them down and for every negative thing written, write a positive way to contest that thought, idea, or situation. The best way to beat the enemy and combat negative thoughts are with the Word (Bible). Find scriptures that speak to your situation and speak them over your life.

### ~The Cry for Attention~

Psalms 145: 17-19 says that God is right in everything He does and filled with kindness. It also goes on to say that God is close to whoever decides to really call on Him. He hears their cry for help and rescues them. If this was God's promise, why couldn't I feel Him close to me? Where was my rescue? All I could see and feel was hurt.

Every time I saw a mom hug her daughter or hold hands it hurt! When I saw mothers and daughters with good relationships it hurt. When I heard daughters call themselves "daddy's girls" I felt hurt. I felt unimportant and under-valued. I had wished so long to be close to my mom or have a dad I was close to but that never happened. I felt like I wouldn't have had the need to seek others out to help me if I had a strong relationship with my mother or father. I, somewhat, blamed my mother and father for my continued urge for seeking attention. What my parents couldn't provide for me, I sought elsewhere. I eventually came to realize how that thought process kept me caged up in my own mind. I was living in a self-made maximum security emotional prison. I was the prisoner, the guard, and the Warden. The interesting thing is that I didn't even realize it at that time.

Every time I'd reach out for help I fell flat on my face. Most of the times I was thrown on my face (figuratively). I was made to feel that I was either too much to deal with, too weird, too friendly, too dishonest, too honest, or just not the typical "happy-go-lucky" young lady. After reaching out so many times without success, I started to feel even more helpless and that feeling of helplessness hurt me to my very core. I felt like my needs and problems outweighed any solution one individual could ever meet. I felt rejected, neglected, and misunderstood.

My cries for help became even more desperate. I started to act out in ways I didn't even want to! I started: making public suicide videos, researching ways to kill myself that didn't hurt too much, publicly lashing out at authority, sitting in church services after dismissal in hopes that someone would help me, watching media that fed into my negative feelings towards church and leadership, and researching ways to numb my feelings of hurt (drugs, alcohol, cutting, and pain medications). I couldn't understand how I could be in a church full of "Holy Spirit – Filled" people and no one could see that I was planning to kill myself in front of the congregation. Yes…I had planned to commit suicide in front of an entire congregation of thousands of people just to make sure everyone knew how much I was hurting. I started to question if the Holy Spirit was even real. I felt so invisible. I felt like I was at the top of a mountain screaming, but no one was willing to hear me. But one things for sure: I was certain they would hear me on that early Sunday morning! I share a bit more about that Sunday morning plan in the following chapter.

My need for attention negatively affected my decisions to participate in unhealthy, perverted relationships and lifestyles. I started fooling around with men and women (married and single). People that were assigned to pray for me were preying on me and I let it happen! Allowing those things to happen gave me a sense of power and displaced value. I was "creeping" with people I had no business messing around with. Can you imagine the amount of power and "specialness" I felt to know that I was sleeping with the pastor's wife and getting all the love and attention I needed? While everyone else was enjoying church service, I would watch her on stage captivating everyone's attention, imagining how our next "hook-up" would play out. It felt good to be in control of something in my life: to have someone thinking about me just as much as I thought about them. I didn't plan for anything like that to happen, but it felt good to know that I had something special I could hold on to. I found pleasure in knowing I could control how her emotions and body reacted to my words and actions. My flesh was pulling me one way while my mind in another. The problem was that I was trying to hold on to something that didn't belong to me and was extremely harmful to my spiritual development. I found an avenue to express my misconstrued love and it cost me my church family, my friends, and almost my life.

I had nothing and found myself accepting any and everything I could get my hands on. My choices caused me to be kicked out of church, drop out of my Doctorate program, be tormented at night, and completely lose myself in this world. I found myself going to clubs in hopes of connecting with anyone. I would drink as often as I could so that I could avoid the feelings of guilt due to my relationship escapades and personal choices. I wanted to make myself hurt, physically and emotionally. I would allow men, who meant me no good, to speak into my ear and take from me what didn't belong to them. Everything I was doing was in hopes that someone would see me spiraling out of control and take the time to ask me if I was okay. I was willing to do the wrong thing to fulfill the right feelings and needs.

I thought myself to be a pretty genuine person with a big heart, but others didn't love the way I did. I loved from a place of fear of rejection and abandonment. I would worry about losing a friend before we even had a chance of building a friendship. I became so fearful of people and relationships that I started to isolate myself from society. I stopped going to church, cut all my friends off, and told God that I was no longer feeling Him as Father or friend. Things got even worse when I decided to cut God out of my life. Any inch of hope that I once had was now gone. I stopped crying out. The things that I found myself doing for attention were no longer helpful or comforting. All they did was leave big gaping holes in my heart. I hated myself. I hated where I was in life. I hated who I had become. Although I made a deliberate choice to shut God and people out of my life I always felt a pulling back to his presence. I started to attend church online and watch different preachers and teachers speak about the love of God. My heart began to open up, once again, to God and I felt the urge to reconnect with Him. It was difficult for me to remain disconnected from my creator.

One day I accidentally started talking to God again after reassuring Him that he meant nothing to me. I had previously made up in my mind that I was going to live life without Him, but that didn't work out too well. I would find myself praying through-out the day and even making little jokes with Him. My prayer went something like this:

"God, what's wrong with me? Where are you? I feel so alone and afraid. I've done too much to come back to you. What are people going to think now? Please find a way to kill me. You're the only one who really gets me. When will I get a break? I didn't ask to be where I am yet you allow me to feel so alone. There are no more people that have your heart anymore. I look around and everyone is trying to find a way out. Pastors are killing themselves. Children are killing themselves. How can you possibly use someone like me? I'm dirty. I'm not authentic. I'm whoever they want me to be. I value people relationships more than the relationship I have with you. I don't think you can do for me more than what another person can. I can't even see you! I can't feel your hug or touch! I don't even know your voice. I'm so broken God, and I don't know what to do. I don't want to live but I don't want to die. What do I do? Why am I even talking to you right now? Who am I kidding? I don't know how to live without you. Help me please before I do something I can't turn back from. Fill the voids that cause me to do stupid stuff. Help me receive your love. I need your love right now. Show me who you are and I'll give up who I'm pretending to be. Dig up my root of rejection and root me in your love. Disconnect me from everything that means to harm me. Protect me, even if it's from myself. I have messed up so many times and I'm tired of going back and forth. Examine my heart and give me a renewed thought process. This can't be how my life plays out. I didn't go through all that stuff to end up dead. Bring me good Christian friends. Send people to pray for me. Send me hugs and kind words. Remove the covering from my eyes that cause me to be blinded from my purpose. I don't know who I am anymore. Remind me. As long as I know it's your voice I'm hearing, I'll do whatever you want me to do. So make your voice clear to me. God, I ask you these things in Jesus name…Amen."

I slowly started to connect with God again. I talked to Him as much as I could remember to. Instead of crying out to the world for attention, I cried out to Him. When I didn't know what to say, I'd just groan and cry. I knew He understood my cry. I began to walk in a peace that could only come from Him. Every now and then I'd see the enemy try his tactics, but God opened my eyes and I learned not to go by what I felt, saw, or heard but by what I believed: And I believed the Word of God and His unconditional love for me. I held onto those facts with everything I had.

Psalms 27:9-10 reminded me that each time I felt like I had no way out and no support, that God would never abandon me! I knew that if He was with me there was a possibility I could defeat the obsession I had with death and its distorted benefits. I wanted to believe. I tried to believe. But doubt and fear was ever present and crippling.

The only thing that made any real sense to me, at this point, was to establish a plan. I needed to do something about what was going on in my life. What that plan was, I had no idea. But doing nothing was no longer an option. I had to either find a way to live or a reason to die. One way or another something had to give…

If we know who or what we are fighting against we can better plan to win that battle. Every good general has a battle plan. The enemy can either be engaged straight on or strategically attacked. Whichever way we decide to approach our battles, a plan must be in place. When there is a lack of sufficient planning, the enemy has an increased chance of wounding or possibly killing the purpose on our lives. There is nothing harder than living a life without purpose and direction.

Ephesians 6:12 talks about who our real enemy is. We don't fight against flesh and blood (or the things we can actually see) but against principalities, powers, rulers of darkness, and spiritual wickedness (the things we cannot see). Well, if we are fighting a battle against some weird entities we cannot see, how can we possibly win? Ephesians 6 speaks of the importance of putting on our armor each day.

This armor helps protect us from the previously stated unseen enemies and better equips us to effectively battle from both the defensive and offensive positions. Our armor and weapons consist of the following: (a) Belt of truth; (b) Breastplate of Righteousness; (c) Helmet of Salvation; (d) Shield of Faith; (e) Sword of Spirit; (f) Gospel of Peace; and (g) Praying in the Spirit.

The belt of truth is standing on the potency of Gods' Word. It's knowing that, without a doubt, scripture is reliable and truthful. The breast plate of righteousness is the covering that cleanses us from guilt through the blood of Jesus Christ. We are ensured that we have the Fathers' forgiveness when we "fall." The helmet of salvation reminds us that we eternally belong to Jesus Christ. Doubt and fear is defeated once we receive the assurance that nothing can separate us from the love of God. The shield of faith extinguishes the arrows (or "bad things") that come at us on a regular basis. The sword of the spirit is both an offensive and defensive weapon. We are able to articulate the Word of God to resist and repel Satan. The gospel of peace is walking in a readiness to resolve conflict and share the message of reconciliation. Wherever division and conflict is, the enemy seeks to exploit those situations. It is beneficial to appropriately deal with or resolve conflicted relationships in our lives. When left unresolved, the enemy can and will find a way to cause problems in those relationships. Finally, praying in the spirit is being intentional about communicating with God. Our prayers are like guided missiles that penetrate enemy strongholds.

So now that we understand the importance of having a plan and effectively utilizing it, living then becomes a beautiful gift instead of a worrisome burden. To value life is to embrace the good, bad, and ugly without wanting to "check-out." It's a choice that only you can make. Whatever your decision, make it knowing that God loves you unconditionally. Everyone else might let you down, but God is nothing like what you experience with human relationships.

# To Live or Not to Live: Activity

What would make you devalue your life?




What makes life worth living?




Have you ever considered "taking a break: from life by means of suicide or any form of hurting yourself? If so, Explain.




What are some ways you cry out for attention? Is it effective?

# ~SELF- REFLECTION~

# PICTURE IT

# CHAPTER 3

## *The Plan*

{Jeremiah 29:11, NLT}

"For I know the plans I have for you, says the Lord. They are plans for good and not for disaster, to give you a future and a hope."

Having a suicide plan is the single most important fact that determines if a person has reached their threshold of "hanging in there." Once an individual begins to plan their death, they have allowed their emotions to manifest into action. Reality no longer exists. The things that might not seem to be a big deal now becomes overbearing and overwhelming. Things no longer make sense. Clarity becomes confusion. There is little to no hope and the capacity of returning to a settled state of mind becomes difficult. Losing hope manifests physically when a person has determined that life no longer offers the necessities of survival. A suicidal person isn't always able to think logically. Expecting them to respond in a manner that makes sense might prove unattainable. But where there is hope there is a chance. Suicide isn't the only plan I conjured up and held on to. There were also plans of incarceration, isolation, and victimization which I address later on in my story.

As a child, I was pretty tough and resilient. I was taught that committing suicide would land me on a front row seat to hell. So I figured that it made no sense for me to live a life of hell then turn around and kill myself and end up right back in hell. Nevertheless, I sat hopelessly in my room one day wiping my eyes, thinking about my lack of friends and recent loss of my virginity. I thought about the hurtful relationships and continued negativity in my life. I remembered the molestation and promiscuity in my young life. When I saw who I had become I was disgusted and ashamed. I felt as though my life had no value and my best efforts to survive my situation had failed. I thought about every person that had ever come into my life and then abandoned me. I imagined a future of loneliness and bitterness. I convinced myself that no one would ever care for me in the way I needed them to and that the pain I was feeling would never go away. Before I knew it, I began to swallow rubbing alcohol as if I were drinking a 16 ounce bottle of water. I was 12 years old but carrying the load of an experienced adult. The taste was bitter and it hurt going down my throat. My ears started to ring as the rubbing alcohol touched the back of my throat. All I remember, after swallowing the alcohol, was waking up in my room. I didn't know how long I had been unconscious or what physically happened to me. I woke up confused and sad. My angel, most definitely, had a full time job keeping up with me! I went through that entire experience without having said one word to anyone. It was only by the grace of God that I survived that dance with death and lived to share the story.

Each time I decided that I was going to kill myself there wasn't much room for planning things out. It was a spur of the moment kind of thing. I just knew that I wanted to die. Any time I pondered on the specifics of how I would kill myself I would usually end up discouraging myself and pressing forward. I'd start thinking about the people I would leave behind and my dog. Who would take care of my dog? Would my nephews recover from my actions? I thought about how bad my car would be damaged if I failed my suicide attempt while driving and how much I would have to pay to fix it. Therefore planning my suicide didn't work out too well for me. But at my lowest points, when I believed that no one could help me, I started to make plans for my exit from earth. I had finally made up in my mind that it was my time and that God would still love me. See…If I could convince myself that dying was a good thing with minimal consequences then I knew that it would be so much easier to finally do it.

Initially, I planned to injure myself bad enough so that I was incapacitated for a good amount of time. I wouldn't be totally dead (yes I just said totally dead as if you can be partially dead), but banged up enough to make sure my voice was heard or at least seen. At the time, that plan felt perfectly acceptable! There was nothing anyone could say to me to make me feel any differently.

Sometimes we can be so deep in pain and confusion that even the unthinkable becomes a possibility. The idea of becoming temporarily injured was connected to my need for love, understanding, acceptance, and validation. There were times I would be driving on the road and instantly think about driving into oncoming traffic. I thought about cutting my wrists, but I didn't want my skin to get scarred. Wait a minute??? Who thinks about their skin being scarred when trying to take their life? I promise you I wasn't a vain person. I was just confused and hurt. I even thought about purposefully getting incarcerated so that I didn't have to be responsible for anything (paying bills, cooking, thinking, mowing my lawn, cleaning the pool, etc.…). I had planned to walk right up to police officers and assault them without any reason! I considered buying a gun and playing Russian roulette with my life. I tried starving myself, but then I got hungry. It's okay…I laughed too when I reread that statement. I just wanted a way out and I was willing to do anything to make that happen. If I could get hurt really bad or be locked up, then just maybe I could get that love and attention I needed. I wasn't too concerned with the other consequences.

One Sunday morning I woke up and got dressed in preparation to attend church, but not for the reasons you might think. I had a plan that I believed would give me the attention and voice I needed. I wasn't a big fan of church due to my negative experiences with leadership but I was tired of suffering in silence. All I could think about was death and sadness. I was self-medicating with alcohol and pain pills but it just wasn't strong enough anymore. I needed some kind of relief. I was a bit intoxicated and confused but I was ready to start planning for my "Big Exit." I had planned to walk up to the altar in front of my church and kill myself in front of the entire congregation. What better stage than this to prove my worth, was what I thought? I had been attending The Faith Center for maybe six or so months off and on. I'd attend one week then stay home for 3-4 weeks. I would stream some of the services online and then disappear for another few weeks. A Minister named Thomas Glass would always check on me and encourage me to attend Discipleship classes and join the music ministry. But I would just smile awkwardly and nod my head and ignore him. It was because of him that I showed up to church the few times that I did. The pastor, Bishop Henry Fernandez was a pretty cool dude. I had initially heard that his church wasn't a good place to grow spiritually and that he was only interested in cleaning out the pockets of his members. But every week I attended I listened to this short, bald-headed, transparent, caring Jamaican man speak life into his members. I never met him, but I understood him. He seemed to have a good heart. The church was so huge! But yet I felt connected to him. I was able to relate to his experiences and he taught in a manner that was easily received and understood. He just appeared to care for his congregation and although he couldn't have a personal relationship with each member he did things to make sure members felt supported and connected with each other and leadership. When he preached his messages it shifted my heart every single time! That day, I initially planned on walking right up to the stage and killing myself in front of the congregation but he began to speak about being aware and sensitive to the needs of people around you. I felt like he was almost defending me and my hurtful experiences! I felt like he understood my hurt. I felt justified about being disappointed with how I had been treated. I felt like I had a voice. Of course it made perfect sense for me to take my life in front of the institution that took so much from me. I couldn't figure out if I was going to shoot myself in the head or cut my wrists or throat. I just wanted to do something dramatic. Instead, I officially joined the church and went to a minister for prayer. No one knew what would've happened that day... but God! The enemy thought he had me but it didn't quite work out that way. I found life and genuine love that day.

Do you see how the enemy can use your mind to turn on itself? It goes to show just how impactful your needs can affect your actions. You'll find yourself living your life from what you lack. What you believe you don't have will impact your behavior towards what you believe you need. Living life from lack is a sure way to end up experiencing a myriad of excess challenges and feelings of decreased value. Although I had gotten past that particular incident, I recalled previous experiences of suicide attempts that made me feel as though I would never stop thinking about dying. I felt helpless. I felt like help couldn't come quick enough to help me in the ways I needed. As quickly as I overcame one experience I was bombarded by another.

A few months previous to the attempted suicide in my church, I woke up one morning after a few minutes of sleep. Yes minutes! That was regular practice for me. My eyes were swollen from crying the night before. I was so depressed. I couldn't afford my mortgage payments. I had no consistent church family (I hadn't been attending

church consistently enough to develop substantial relationships). My friends were completely oblivious to my situation. My dog kept getting sick. My pool would not stay blue (anyone who owns a pool understands this struggle)! I was broke, hungry, and overweight. Anything that could go wrong was going wrong in my life. That was it! I walked to my guest room and swallowed a bottle of high-dosage pain pills without thinking twice. I sat on my coach and waited to die. I waited and waited and, still, nothing. I even started watching an episode of "Power" while waiting to die. Out of nowhere I started to feel groggy and my speech became slurred. I realized that this might be it. My dog calmly placed his head on my lap and I put my head back waiting for the room to stop spinning. My cell phone was in my hand as I remembered all the people that had let me down. I began to hum a song to myself and by the time I finished humming the song I called a friend. Within a few minutes she was at my home talking to me. I told her what happened and she suggested I try to vomit. That didn't work out too well. I just couldn't activate my gag reflex on purpose! She stayed with me for hours and talked to me. I'm glad to let you know that I didn't die! I began to feel hope again. I felt like just maybe I could make it. That was the last physical attempt I ever made on my life, but it wouldn't be the last time thoughts of suicide entered my mind. There was always a constant battle for my life. Each time I experienced victory, misery was waiting for me around the bend. I wasn't at a point where I had figured out a consistent way to address my concerns and issues without placing my life in jeopardy, but I wanted to be.

On three separate occasions I found myself institutionalized in mental hospitals: Once as a child and two times as an adult. I remember, as a child, being restrained in a strait jacket for not being compliant with staff. I laid on a cold bench afraid and hurt wishing I could be held in the arms of someone that loved me. But I never allowed my fear to show on my face or in my response. I made sure they knew that they couldn't control me even in my restraints. The lights were bright and a single camera panned the room, moving whenever I moved. The atmosphere was cold and calculated. Anything I was feeling became intensified. I was so alone and misunderstood. I couldn't understand why any of this was happening to me!

My experience, as an adult, was much different. I witnessed people walking around like medicated zombies. I felt so out of place. Being in that environment fueled my will to die even more. "I just had to pretend I was okay long enough to be released," was what I told myself. I had one friend who checked up on me and brought me extra clothes during my observation process. She was my best friend. Well, she was kind of my only friend. Being in mental hospitals forever changed the way I sought help and verbalized my concerns. I never again told anyone that I had a plan to die. I learned to internalize everything and mask anything that reared its head externally. No crying! No speaking! No feeling! I realized that mental hospitals couldn't help me so I became extremely violent. I fought everybody for anything. I would fight in church, at school, and at home. I fought my mother, siblings, peers, strangers, and whoever else dared to challenge me in anything. Eventually, that behavior lead down a path to another type of institutionalization.

As a teenager, I found myself locked up in juvenile detention center and charged with "attempted assault with a deadly weapon." I had gotten into a verbal altercation with one of my stepdads and he proceeded to slam me on the floor. I wasn't having it! I ran to the kitchen and found the biggest knife I could! That fool was about to die! After a few threats and explicit vernacular, the police was called to my home. The police came into my home with their guns pointed at my head, knowing nothing about my living situation. She yelled! "Put the knife down!" I dropped the knife and laid down on my stomach. She kneeled in my back and handcuffed me so tightly that I couldn't feel my fingers. I still remember the pain of her knees being in my back as she placed handcuffs on my little hands. I spent 3 days in juvenile detention center. Sure enough, I enjoyed my stay. I made many friends and I felt more loved in that facility than I did at home. I was really only concerned about one thing while serving time in juvenile detention center. I remember being concerned about the class work I was missing in school. See, at my school, if your grades were great in each class you wouldn't have to take any exams. There was nothing in this world that was going to separate me from my exam exemptions! I was released after three days and my record was expunged. I had never gotten in trouble with the law before and the judge felt as though I could be reformed. But the pain I felt from life followed me wherever I went.

I tried everything I could think of to numb my pain: alcohol, sex, medication, masturbation, isolation, procrastination, incarceration, violence, victimization, lying, running, hiding, cutting, leaving the church, and so many other harmful things, but none of them availed. With each bad decision I made I felt the emotional, physical, and spiritual consequences. I welcomed the pain with open arms. See, for me, it was better to feel pain than nothing at all. The pain gave me a reason to hold on to every bad experience and illogical ideology. The pain became the drive behind all of my actions. It soothed the cravings I had for attention. The pain reminded me of how easily life could be devalued. How does one avoid allowing negative life experiences to adversely impact who they become? Each experience left, both, visible and hidden scars. Sometimes it felt as though I had so many scars that no one could see who I really was. At times, I was unsure of who I had become myself. I became whatever my environment needed me to be at the time. If I needed to be a rape victim I played it well. If I had to be an abused child, I walked in every aspect of who that was. If I had to be the friend with overwhelming issues and challenges, I embraced every moment of it. I refused to let go of those hurtful experiences because holding on to them meant receiving love, avoiding rejection, and being justified in my reactions and responses.

I needed something real to happen in my life. The only option I hadn't tried on a consistent basis was God. I'd hear people say how awesome He was and the benefits of connecting with Him. People would talk about experiencing His glory and presence but I just didn't see what they saw. What glory? What presence? How did it feel? Did it have a look? Was I even worthy of it? Why would I choose to connect to an entity that I couldn't even see? Being cool with Him (Jesus) meant that I had to walk by faith. It meant I had to put my trust in another person or thing that may or may not even be real. That wasn't a risk I wanted to take but I had tried everything else and none of them worked. I started to wonder if maybe Jesus had a plan for me that could help bring me out of the hole I was buried in. I was being buried alive. I was losing ground and I needed something to happen in my life.

So many different plans played out in my life, but only Gods plan remained, whether or not I wanted to completely believe in Him. He used every situation for my good. As soon as I gave Him a real chance, He blew my mind. I had given Him some fake chances before so having completely opened up to Him and trusting Him was a choice I was unfamiliar with.

My plan was not God's plan. He had so much more in store for me. If you're reading this very sentence right now, God was able to use my twisted mind and experiences to do His work. Until you have finished what God intended for you to do here on earth, you cannot escape the purpose and destiny on your life. Someone needs to hear your story. Someone needs to know your pain and how you got through. Giving up can't be your only option. Just maybe you can hold on a little longer. Try God out and allow Him to take what the devil meant for evil and turn it around for your good.

You don't have to be the victim to get what you need from Him or others. The very fact you survived the thought of suicide or any other life challenge proves that you have the will and ability, through Christ, to make it through. When you find yourself thinking about death or dying recognize how important your life is to those around you. If the enemy feels the need to try and kill you there must be something powerful you were destined to accomplish. We all have a choice. We can choose life or we can choose death. We overcome by the word of our testimony. Share your thoughts, feelings, and concerns with someone. Share them with God! It might seem pointless, but what do you have to lose?

My plan was clearly laid out. I had placed everything together, detail by detail, in hopes of accomplishing my distorted plan of death. My plan kind of sucked, but I was tired and hurt. Life had nothing to offer me and I needed a way out. The moment I yielded myself to God, He took my disastrous plans and created a master piece. Yielding to God was the best decision I could ever make. Doing so allowed me to walk in a freedom I had never experienced before. The situations that use to appear hopeless became helpful. It's as if a cover was removed from my eyes and I could finally see the light. I began to wonder how life would be from the stance of a victor instead of a victim. It was so easy to be a victim and I was well within in my rights to feel that way. But I often felt as though a greater impact could take place if I walked as a survivor instead of a victim. We don't always have a choice in what we experience but we usually have a choice in how we respond. It's in that response that we can begin to really find out who we are and what we can do to impact our environment.

How do you want to impact your environment? Do you want to be remembered as a victim or survivor? What's the legacy you want to leave behind? Whoever hurt you and however they did it: Is it worth your life? What are you willing to do to survive your situation? Think about these questions. Answer them and if you find that you have some fight left in you, keep on fighting! Everyone won't cross the finish line of life but you have the power to shift your experience and walk in an authority that commands your will to line up with the will of God. This world needs you. And no matter what it seems like, your testimony can help save so many more lives. Ask God what His plans are for your life and ask Him to position and prepare you for purpose. Because it's in purpose that you'll find peace.

# The Plan: Activity

Have you ever found yourself planning to do something that would negatively impact your life? If so, what was your plan and how did it play out?

Have you ever successfully planned an effective method to address negative thoughts or experiences? If so, Explain. If not, make one now. (Ex: breathing, beach, journaling, writing poetry, etc…)

If you could ask God to change the plans for your life, what would you ask Him to do?

Note: Share the answers of your previous questions with someone that can pray for you.

# ~SELF-REFLECTION~

# PICTURE IT

# CHAPTER 4

## *Victim or Victor*

{Isaiah 53:5, NLT}

"But he was pierced for our rebellion, crushed for our sins. He was beaten so we could be whole. He was whipped so we could be healed."

I was addicted to being a victim. Being a victim came with so many benefits. As a victim, I was entitled to sympathy and attention, or at least that's what I believed. In my world, receiving sympathy meant I would be given more attention and love. It didn't matter, to me, if the love was conditional, temporary, unreal, or perverted. I'd take whatever I could get! I was okay with a rub on the back or an "Oh you poor thing" comment or even a look of pity. I lived for those type of responses and when I didn't get it I created situations that made sure I would receive them. For example: I was feeling down one day. I can't remember all the specifics of what happened but I remembered feeling so alone, depressed, and sad. I thought about the fact that I was an older (no way I'm telling my age) unmarried woman without children and started to wonder if something was wrong with me! I was beautiful, smart, and ambitious but felt like I was tainted because everyone else around me was married with children and I wasn't. I was always the bridesmaid but never the bride. What good were my college degrees and ambition if I had no one to share them with? Well, I didn't think that was a good enough reason to be unhappy and suicidal so I created a more sympathetic situation. I decided to drive my car to a park and sit in the parking lot for hours. I totally convinced myself that I should drive into a close by lake. I continuously sought out ways to create havoc in my life. Once I convinced myself that I wanted to die, I called a friend and drew them into my situation. What started out as a night of just being disappointed with where I was in life turned into an all-out crisis! I was so use to being a victim that I lived for the thrill of sympathetic responses. I was willing to say and do anything to get what I needed (love and attention). Admitting that was so hard because in

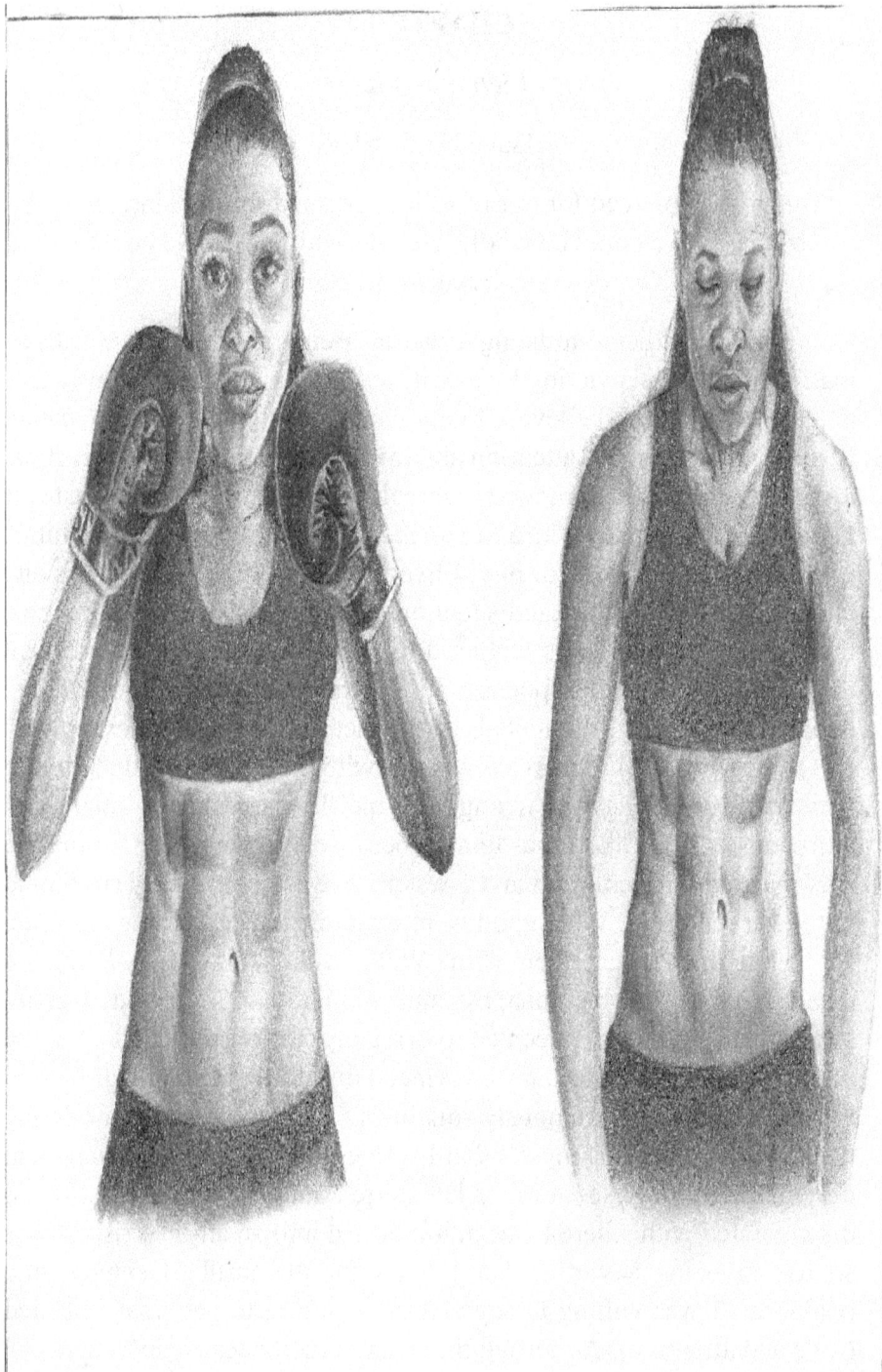

doing so it put the pressure back on me. It meant that I had to become accountable for my actions and I didn't want to accept that!

As a victim, it ensured that I didn't have to take responsibility for any of my actions. After all, what person could blame me for feeling the way I did? I felt like I had every right to grovel in my victimization. No one could tell me I wasn't a victim because they hadn't been through what I had experienced. As a victim, I could freely feel sorry for myself. I was able to hold grudges and be unforgiving. I could have outbursts and tantrums that were justified by my emotional and physical experiences. I was more familiar with being a victim than a victor. Walking as a victor was too unknown for me. Who would accept me as a victor? What fun was that? I didn't mean to think this way, but I had gone through life without anyone really giving me the opportunity to speak my story so I felt the need to relive my story over and over until I felt as though someone understood my feelings. I wasn't allowed to grieve my childhood. I lost so many things and when you go through life just losing and losing without the opportunity to reflect and respond it's easy to get stuck in that moment of life. I was stuck being a victim and I liked it. But it took a lot of work and energy to maintain my victimization. The process that was necessary for me to overcome my victimization was halted with distraction after distraction. I use to wish anyone would cry for me. I wanted someone to empathize with the hurt I had been put through and I believed that being a victim would give me the best chance of that happening. I did have one friend that sat down with me one day and cried with and for me. I had never experienced anything like that before. I had never seen the concern for myself in someone else's eyes. I felt as though I needed that experience to occur a few more times before I could completely let go of being a victim. I just wasn't ready.

There were some draw backs to being a victim. As a victim I couldn't healthily get through my storms or trials. I was also more prone to attacks from the enemy. See, a victim depends on others for their happiness and survival. Depending on others made it so much easier for chaos, manipulation, and regret to coexist in relationships. Victimization caused instability in my mind, pain in my body, and hate

49

in my heart. I could never truly be who God created me to be because I was too caught up accepting what my offenders tried to make me become. I was fueled by anger, pride, self-righteousness, and rebellion. I was more interested in pleasing people than God. I hated authority. As a matter of fact, I still struggle with submitting to authority. Submission, in my mind, meant allowing myself to potentially be hurt or victimized. Submission meant I was weak and unable to take control of any situation. Being a victim came with constant reminders of disappointment, regret, and self-condemnation. I wanted to try something new and different. My method of dealing with challenges wasn't really getting me anywhere. I often wondered how things might be for me if I walked as a victor or survivor.

On the other hand, being a victor meant taking responsibility for my actions. It meant that I would have to experience healing and deliverance in the areas of my life that I wanted to hold on to and suppress. Walking in total freedom meant I would have to forgive and let go of people and situations that I had no control over. Letting go, in my mind, meant that I would have nothing left for me to hold on to. I had lost so much already: my innocence, my mind at times, my friends, my mother, my father, my siblings, and myself. Being a victor required me to be too responsible. I felt like being a victor meant no more crying, sadness, neediness, and inconsistency. I felt those things were necessary in order for me to be relevant, understood, and justified. It took me a long time to choose the victor over the victim. Doing so stretched my faith and my fight. I learned quickly that you could still cry as a victor. Just because you choose to be a victor doesn't devalue your experience. Being a victor doesn't provide a pass for those who hurt you. You are entitled to feel and experience your circumstance however you need to. You don't have to forget but you do need to forgive.

Walking as a victor allowed me to share my testimony from a healthy place. I could preach, teach, and worship from a more empowered state of mind. Being a victor didn't mean that I couldn't be justified in how I felt. Instead, it made my justification the driving force behind my reunification with my Creator (God). When I was able to reconnect with the person that knew and loved me the most, I was able to better understand why I had experienced the things I did and how I could use those experiences to bring others closer to Christ. I decided that God wasn't that bad of a dude. I remember always thinking to myself how God could allow bad things to happen to innocent people. That just didn't seem fair. Here's what I learned. God gives everyone choices. Sometimes the bad choices of one person can infringe on the good choices of someone else. Another person's mistake or intentional misuse of power can interfere with your good decisions and circumstances. But even when situations like that happen, God will use the very same situation to bring Him glory. What that means is that the good, bad, and ugly in our lives can still create a beautiful story. What was meant to hurt you could very well be what propels you into purpose. God is that attentive and caring that He will not allow any of your experiences to be "wasted."

Take a listen to this analogy and try to imagine how you can apply it to your life. Think about the different ingredients in a cake. I'm not much of a cook (as a matter of fact, I'm pretty bad) but I believe the main ingredients are: flour, sugar, butter, milk, and eggs. If you were to taste or remove one of those ingredients from the cake it would probably taste pretty bad. But when they are strategically combined, a sweet aroma fills the kitchen and your mouth begins to salivate at the taste of that cake. We should view our different experiences and challenges in a similar manner. Each experience, when viewed by itself, seems pretty hurtful and meaningless. But when you put all the experiences together they create this beautiful story called your life. They help build something called your testimony. You choose how you allow your experiences to influence your life.

## <u>Victim or Victor: Activity</u>

What do you believe are the characteristics of a victim? Do you recognize any of those character traits in yourself?

Was there ever a point in your life where you felt as though you were forced to be a victim? Explain.

Have you ever felt like a victor or survivor? If so, what do you believe are the benefits of approaching life as a survivor/victor? If not, what do you believe stops you from experiencing life from a victor stance?

# ~SELF-REFLECTION~

# <u>PICTURE IT</u>

# CHAPTER 5

## *The Root*

{1 Corinthians 3:7, NLT}

"It's not important who does the planting, or who does the watering. What's important is that God makes the seed grow."

Through-out my life there was a lack of stability, reliability, consistency, and connectivity. I wanted so much to be wanted, valued, and liked. I wanted to be someone's special person. I'd hear people say that I was special to God, but everyone is considered special to God, so for me that wasn't really the same validation I was looking for. I wanted love that didn't come with an expiration date. I wanted love that others could see me receiving.

I wanted to know that I could be angry or disappointed with someone, express how I felt and they would still be a part of my life afterwards. Things were always so final in my home and community. Every time I made a mistake or acted out, I was rejected. I was called names and ignored. People laughed and mocked me. It was so hard for me to understand how people couldn't love unconditionally, because it was so easy for me to exemplify. When my stepdads were molesting me, I stuck around. When family members touched me inappropriately, I loved them just the same. I accepted the unacceptable, so why couldn't someone accept me? I learned quickly that I should never display negative feelings to someone I loved or I would risk the chance of being rejected. This ideology was rooted in the very being of who I was and I didn't know how to uproot it by myself.

As I stated earlier, I was a pretty good student athlete. While playing basketball I became really close with one of my coaches. We were friends for many years. She always looked out for me and made sure I was successful in whatever I did. When I didn't have new "back-to- school" clothes and shoes, she took me shopping. She styled my hair. She attended my graduations and I am the godmother to one of her children. My coach had my back even when she knew I was a total mess. I have no idea why she never called me out on my mess but it

made me a better individual. She treated me like a sister. I would hang out with her family on the weekends and spend quality time learning how to be successful without adapting to what others felt I should be. That relationship taught me how to love people past their faults. But one day we got into a big argument. I said some pretty mean things and just like that….the woman I loved and admired for so long was out of my life and remained out of my life for over 10 years. I couldn't understand how I could be so easily rejected and disconnected from someone that played such a vital role in my life. For years, the breaking of that friendship bothered me. It reinforced my mindset that I could never respond emotionally or without thought because doing so would mean the end of important relationships.

REJECTION was my root! It was the driving force behind every response, reaction, and experience in my life. I was afraid to experience it. I felt as though my family, friends, and coaches all rejected me at some point in my life. I even accused God of turning His back on me at some point. Why else did I have such a rough up-bringing and so many years of difficulty?

### ~Revelation~

One day I asked God what my root was and He said, "Rejection." I asked because I wanted to approach my root head on so that I could stop wanting to dance with death. I was tired of wanting to die if someone breathed on me too hard. Every response I had was dramatic. Where someone else might get mad and walk away from the situation, I wanted to walk away from life! What made me so overly sensitive? For me it was rejection. For someone else it could be: abandonment, hopelessness, neglect, low self-esteem, pride, un-forgiveness, or perversion, to name a few.

There came a point where I made up in my mind that I was finished with attending church, participating in ministry, and confiding in people. I wanted nothing to do with connecting to another living soul. I viewed people as being natural pitfalls and wasted expectations. Whenever I depended on a person for happiness, comfort, or peace I ended up experiencing hurtful let-downs. Furthermore, I had decided that I was no longer going to attend church anymore because of the actions of people. It wasn't anything that God had done to me that kept me from His church, but the actions of His people.

I ended up having a conversation with one of the praise team leaders, Natasha. She shared with me the importance of not allowing people to affect my relationship with the church and, more importantly, God. She shared some bits of her life experiences and God used her to help me grasp two very important concepts, which forever changed my mindset for the better: People will fail you, but God never will and no matter what happens in life, my actions can never be based on people-experiences, but my God-relationship. Emotionally, I was never the same. God changed my heart and mind and I've been rolling with Him ever since.

I had to pinpoint my source and focus on my real issues. After identifying the source I envisioned what I could do about it. I couldn't take back the years of rejection I had experienced, but I could make sure each new experience was not based on my fear of rejection. I realized that I didn't have to be fearful of rejection from people when I had a God that would never leave or forsake me. It was vital that I be free from people. I couldn't allow the thoughts and actions of an individual to impact my character. What they did shouldn't impact who I was and it definitely shouldn't cause me to devalue my life.

I realized that I didn't really want to die. I just wanted to experience the sincerity, love, appreciation, and acceptance that came with a traumatic event such as death. I wanted to experience the emotional correlations linked with death: the pity, socialization, thoughtfulness, kind words, and attention. I wanted someone to hurt the way I had been hurting. I was willing to die just to be heard. Our emotions can sometimes keep us out of the will of God and, in this case, it kept me from finding peace with wanting to live.

God had to uproot rejection and replant love and acceptance so that my life could blossom and therefore bare sweet fruit. I was tired of the bitter fruit I was baring. You can tell a lot about a person by who they associate with and the fruit of their labor. When I began to examine my fruit, I was horrified. I had to find a way to begin to spring forth sweet fruit in and around my life. I had to shift my focus from pain to perseverance. God made it clear to me that you don't get sentenced to pain. You get trusted with pain. Not everyone can handle something as challenging as having suicidal thoughts. That is literally a life or death situation. If you can find a way to pull through you can help another person get through. You cannot allow your past pain to interrupt your present legacy.

Genuine pain yields genuine reactions, responses, and respect. When you are able to directly relate to the hurtful experiences of others, your impact is so much more relevant and received. Not many people have successfully dealt with outrageous suicidal thoughts and lived to tell the story. Each time you overcome a crisis, another group of people get to hear your victorious story and are better able to pull through their situations. In this world, bad things will happen. It's inevitable! But imagine how much better this world would be if God could use you to help bring joy, empathy, understanding, and love to those debilitating situations. Death doesn't bring peace. Death doesn't bring joy. It doesn't erase your hurt. Instead, death brings chaos, sadness, and pain. It will appear to be the easy way out but there is an easier way out…GOD…

## The Root: Activity

What do you believe is your root? What fuels your response to life situations? (Pray and ask God to reveal this root to you)

What caused that root to manifest or develop in your life? (Think about where the seed/idea could have been planted in your life).

Challenge: Find someone you can share your root with and talk about ways you can change your thought process. It is important to identify your root

# ~SELF-REFLECTION~

# <u>PICTURE IT</u>

# CHAPTER 6

## *Purpose Provides Perseverance*

### {Isaiah 41: 9-10, AMP}

"You whom I [the Lord] have taken from the ends of the earth, And called from its remotest parts And said to you, 'You are My servant, I have chosen you and have not rejected you [even though you are exiled]. 'Do not fear [anything], for I am with you; Do not be afraid, for I am your God. I will strengthen you, be assured I will help you; I will certainly take hold of you with My righteous right hand [a hand of justice, of power, of victory, of salvation]."

Why do we go through the things we do in life? What helps us to persevere despite what we experience? What's the difference between someone who gives up and the person that fights to the finish? These are questions I began to ask myself regularly. In those answers I was able to find strength and encouragement. I had to learn to encourage myself and find ways to persevere even when it felt like my world was falling apart. There's a saying: "You can't make someone that's not hungry eat." When I became desperate enough to persevere beyond my challenges I found the courage to fight back, spiritually.

I think about Jesus and the tough task He had of coming down to earth and dying for our sins. It couldn't have been that easy to know that you were going to get beaten, betrayed, and die on a cross for people that really didn't even appreciate you all that much. How did He physically and mentally prepare for something like that? I know that He was both God and human, but that's some serious stuff! I think about getting a flu shot and question whether or not it's worth not getting sick. But what Jesus had to carry was so heavy. Jesus knew His purpose! He knew the consequences if He had given up. He knew the risks associated with failure. I'm sure He probably thought about His end goal and held on as tight as He could to His purpose so that He could push forward. That couldn't have been easy, no matter who you are. I had to find a way to discover and walk in the purpose God had for me. For me, that process started in my personal prayer time, studying the Word, and participating in the different ministries at my church.

Attending a Mega Church seemed like it was going to be a challenge for me, initially. I had already experienced so much church hurt and was concerned about being unable to make genuinely necessary connections. I couldn't see how I was going to experience healing in a place where I'd be seen as just another face. But God, in his infinite grace and mercy, saw fit to connect me with a powerful prayer warrior, Minister Darlene Hord. I didn't know, initially, that connecting with her would help boost my spiritual experience to another level. I ended up participating in the School of the Prophets (of the Henry Fernandez Institute) and completing Darlene's mentorship program, Daughters of Zion/ Woman of Destiny. In doing so I experienced a spiritual make over that changed me internally and externally.

I found myself being more open to experiencing healing from "church hurt", abuse, and corrupt leadership. I began to deal with others more gently and Christ-like. I was no longer double-minded in my thoughts and I loved others as Christ loved me. One day I realized that my internal changes started to affect my outward appearance. I went from wearing men clothing and being unkempt to dressing more feminine and taking better care of myself. This physical transition was an outward expression of what God was doing in my heart. He used Minister Darlene to help me transition from "raggedy" to rejuvenated. I love that woman to life! Her obedience helped propel me to my purpose.

I only wish there were more people like this in the church. There are so many hurting individuals who just need a word or maybe some time. God placed us on this earth to be fruitful, not busy. The act of one person helped me minister to thousands. Imagine how many more lives could be saved if more people took the time to love and listen instead of focusing on self. I am a living witness that God will use whomever and whatever to get His work done!

I wasn't sure why I had gone through all the things I went through, but I knew that God purposed me. I knew that my story could help someone else. I knew that my love was made to soften the hearts of His children. I went through to help others come through. That's all the reason I needed. As long as people have choices in this world, bad things are going to happen to good people. So in God's infinite love and compassion for us, He uses even the bad to help bring about the good.

With every situation and challenge I experienced I asked God how I could use it to make the world a better place. I asked Him to show me ways to utilize my situation to become a better person. Every molestation, rape, rejection, set-back, punch, slap, hit, confinement, and terror: I found ways to utilize those experiences positively in my life and in the life of others. I couldn't write this book if I hadn't gone through some of these things. I couldn't be so compassionate about the feelings of others if I hadn't felt that same hurt. My experiences made room for my entrance! What should've killed me pushed me into destiny. I faced my fears head on so that they couldn't sneak up on me and take me out. I used my fears and failures as stepping stools.

I use to be afraid of building relationships. Building relationships, for me, meant that I would eventually be disappointed and hurt. I was in bondage with people. I didn't get excited about anything! People caused me to feel the way I did and so the enemy would constantly use others to keep me bound. See, it's nearly impossible to control the actions of others. But I could control my response. Makes sense right? So I tried something new. It wasn't easy at first, but after a few tries I got it! I finally learned how to be free from people. Guess what my solution was? GOD. Sounds a bit cliché right? I can only speak my truth. I knew that He would never leave me or forsake me. He was the only person I could 100% count on to be consistent and always have my best interest in mind. So, I started talking to Him a bit more and reading my bible. I shifted my focus from people to Jesus. I was intentional about sharing EVERYTHING with Him. How could the enemy use what no longer held me in bondage? Ha! Got'em! I mean…people's actions sometimes made me shake my head or maybe suck my teeth, but it no longer drove me into depression and sadness. That was too much power for another individual to have over me. I've been living free ever since and so can you! Initially, I thought that plan was kind of lame, but God "wowed" me and He continues to "wow" me. I was so fascinated from the pleasure and purpose I found in simply talking to Him and spending time in His Word. Guess what else happened in the midst of all that? I accidentally found joy! I wasn't even looking for it! I became happy and no person was able to take that from me! It was mine to keep. The world didn't give it so they couldn't take it away.

Psalms 103:8 says: "The Lord is merciful and gracious, slow to anger and abounding in compassion *and* lovingkindness (AMP)." I found sweet peace in knowing that God's grace would keep me and that He loved me more than I could ever imagine. Scriptures seemed like they would float off of the bible page and wrap around my heart and mind. His Word held me like a mother holds her new born baby. I asked for wisdom and my eyes were opened. I asked for strength and I was able to carry the things I could never carry before (hurt, disappointment, betrayal, etc...).

I learned to have and set appropriate boundaries and expectations. No one person could be there for me 24/7, although I wished they could. People have their own lives. It's not to say that you or I don't deserve great friends or the right to depend on someone else. God made us to be social beings. We need to connect. I just learned that people connections don't make me who I am and they don't determine what I do. People will fail (not always on purpose). And when they failed, I couldn't allow it to affect me so much that I had no will to live, no hope, and no joy. It couldn't affect my joy because they didn't give it to me! No one can take from you what God provides for you. I started to eat more healthily and go to bed at a decent hour. Half of my problems were solved by me simply going to bed! We need rest. The body has to regenerate. Even Jesus rested. I surrendered to God and it was the best decision I ever made. Building a relationship with Jesus revealed to me how I could walk and remain in purpose.

Having purpose can change the way you experience situations. Purpose changes mindsets. Purpose provides! Knowing who you are and what God thinks about you has enough power to change your outlook on life. Purpose provides focus and encouragement. It better allows you to go through your refining process so that you can be made pure as gold. The enemy doesn't want you to walk in purpose. He wants you to be confused and lost. But you do not have to walk in confusion. The bible tells you who you are and just in case you have forgotten, let me remind you.

You are:

1. Complete in Him (Colossians 2:10)
2. Far from oppression and fear doesn't come near you (Isaiah 54:14)
3. Without lack because God supplies all your needs (Philippians 4:19)
4. Able to do all things through Christ who strengthens you (Philippians 4:13)
5. More than a conqueror (Romans 8:37)
6. An overcomer by the blood of the lamb and the word of your testimony (Revelation 12:11)
7. The righteousness of God in Jesus Christ (2 Corinthians 5:21)
8. The head and not the tail; above and not beneath (Deuteronomy 28:13)
9. Light of the world (Matthew 5:14)
10. Forgiven of all your sins and washed in the blood (Ephesians 1:7)
11. Delivered from the power of darkness (Colossians 1:13)
12. Healed by His stripes (Isaiah 53:5)
13. Greatly loved by God (Ephesians 2:4)
14. Are not lacking because God supplies all your needs (Philippians 4:19)

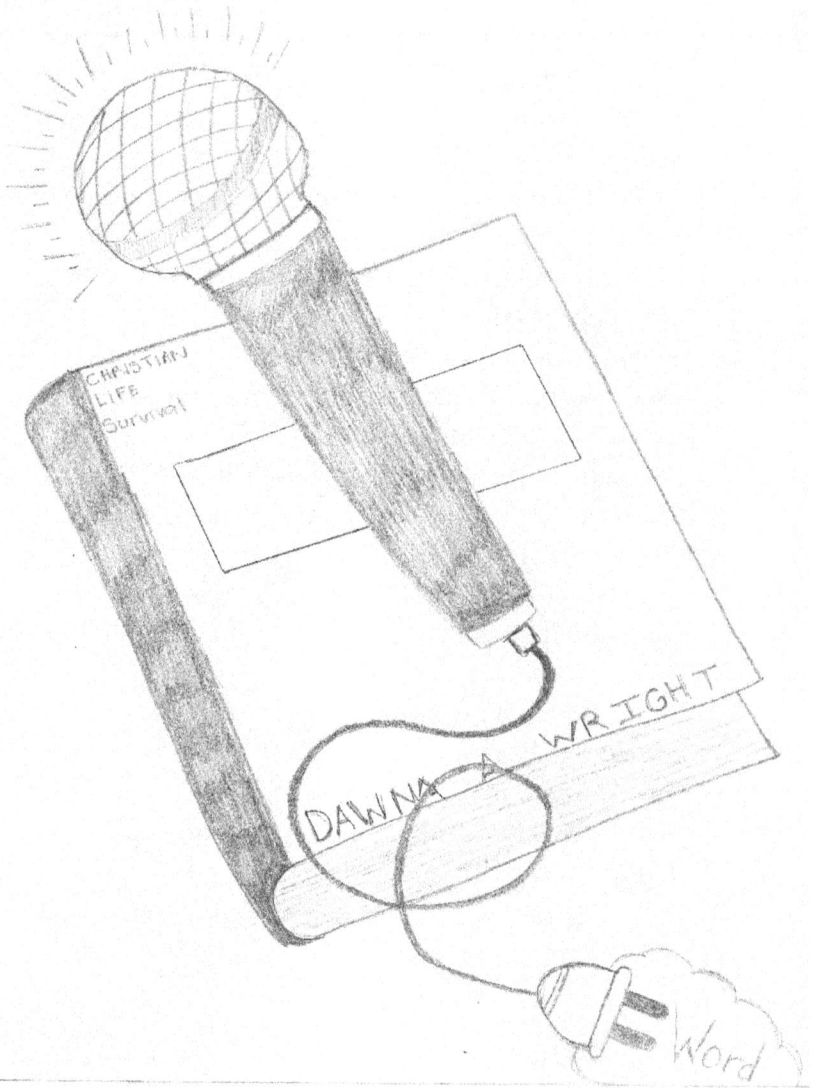

# Purpose: Activity

Do you know what your purpose is? If so, what? If not, ask God.

What are you most passionate about? (What would you do for free?)

Challenge: Ask God what your purpose is (if you don't already know) and write it down. Once you determine your purpose, begin to walk in it.

# ~SELF-REFLECTION~

# PICTURE IT

# CHAPTER 7

## *The Help*

{Luke 10:19, NLT}

"Look, I have given you authority over all the power of the enemy,
and you can walk among snakes and scorpions and crush them.
Nothing will injure you."

Often times, a person that experiences suicidal thoughts will be able to verbalize what they need (emotionally, physically, or spiritually). Helping such a person doesn't require any kind of special training or anointing. It simply requires love, understanding, and good listening skills. People won't always remember what you say but they will remember how you made them feel. There are no magic answers or actions. Responding just requires being genuine and observant. The person who struggles with suicidal thoughts and actually says something about how they're feeling wants to be heard. That person saying something is a great thing, contrary to popular belief, because it means there is still hope. Voicing a need for help does not mean that person isn't seriously considering suicide. It just means that they are able to recognize what's happening and respond effectively. There are people who use threats of suicide as a form of manipulation, but even those individuals should be taken seriously. A person willing to make threats about taking their life to make a point can become extremely dangerous. Many times a situation like this can be diffused by making a choice to listen to whatever needs to be said and addressing feelings before facts. Unfortunately, I was once that person and it is not pleasant for ANYONE! A desperate person will do desperate things to validate their experience.

There isn't one particular characteristic of a person struggling with suicide. Everyone experiences difficulties differently. No two persons will respond in the exact same manner. With every experience comes diverse responses. Suicide doesn't have a universal response or reason. Sometimes it can happen without notice and other times you can see it coming as clear as day. Suicide is no respecter of person, position, or circumstance. Each individual circumstance should be treated with sensitivity, caution, wisdom, and love.

It is important to approach sensitive situations with compassion and concern. Where there is hope, there is a chance of survival. Continue to reach out for help, whether you're the afflicted or affected. If considering suicide or helping someone who is contemplating suicide there are numerous ways to seek additional help. You can talk to a friend, a minister, a pastor, a family member, a professional, specialty groups, or any other available resources.

As I struggled with suicidal thoughts, I had to remember that I was not alone. There were others who were experiencing thoughts of suicide just like me and just because the thoughts occurred didn't mean I was any less valuable to God, the community, or the church. More people battle with thoughts of suicide than meets the eye. My dance with death failed. Whether or not you find yourself dancing with death or observing someone else's dance, know that the battle is already won! The enemy (Satan) will make you believe that suicide is the only way out. He will try to convince you that your death is more profitable than your life. He wants you to feel like nothing. But just because he suggests those thoughts doesn't mean you have to embrace it. Greater is He that is in you than he that is in the world (1 John 4:4).

The best way to win the battle of the mind is to build a solid relationship with Jesus. Getting to know Jesus kind of works the same way as getting to know a close friend. When getting to know a friend you might find yourself hanging out, talking, and just spending quality time together. The more you spend time with your friend the closer you tend to grow with each other. Well, building a relationship with Jesus works the same way. Spend time in His word. Talk to Him like you would a friend. Hang out with Him as much as you can. You'll find that His presence becomes soothing to your situations. I guarantee you this: the more time you spend with God, the less impact negative situations have on your life! After building a solid relationship with God, I asked Him to send me some good God-fearing friends that I could hang out with and connect to. I was very specific in my request but I asked according to His will. Would you know that Jesus gave me the most loving, considerate, passionate, and loyal friends ever? I was able to say what I was experiencing without fear of my information reaching every media outlet by the following day. God strategically placed different individuals in my life for different reasons (Ministers, Prayer Warriors, Business Owners, Leaders, Pastors, Teachers, Prophets, Healers, Evangelists, etc…). I had and continue to have an overflow of supportive individuals in my life. Gods' timing and our timing might not necessarily line up all the time but know that He is working things out for your good. That's not just a famous quote. It's real life!

I want to share this last story with you that helped change the way I processed life's challenges. One day I was walking my beautiful black and tan miniature pinscher dog around the block. He is all of 12 pounds but believes he is so much bigger and stronger than he really is. He has no idea that most cats are bigger than him. But I love him with all my heart. I love to come home to his excitement and loyalty. His little tail wags fast with joy as he jumps on his hind legs trying to share his excitement with me. Every time I come home I take him outside immediately to get some fresh air. This time I decided to take him for a little adventure around the block.

It was about 95 degrees outside and the sun was blazing hot! I decided that I was going to take Buddy (my dog) around the block one time to make sure he remained healthy and strong. About 40% into our walk Buddy began to pant heavily and scurry to find shade. I knew how much further we had to go so I kept pulling on his leash for him to keep going. I was also aware of all the shaded spots along the route that Buddy could take rest under, but all Buddy knew was that he was hot and couldn't go on. He found a shaded spot as we tried to continue our walk and refused to walk any further. He laid down on the grass looking me in the eyes as if to say, "There is no way I'm taking one more step. Help me please." I knew his journey was almost finished but he couldn't see past his current situation. He couldn't think past the burning heat he was experiencing. So being the caring dog owner I am, I picked him up in my arms, loved on him, covered him up, and carried him some of the way. He knew that I wouldn't leave him or cause him to walk in what he believed he was incapable of walking in or through. After I saw that he had gotten enough rest and cooled down a bit I placed him back on his feet to finish the rest of the walk. He needed to go through his walking process to build his endurance so that he could be strong and healthy. He also had to be familiar with his territory should he ever become lost. (Whew! That is a word for someone)

This caused me to think about how God sees where we are going in life. He knows every shaded area along our path. He knows when things are too much to bare. He knows why we need to go through different challenges and situations. He has the power to lift us up and carry us when we can't carry ourselves. Life sometimes becomes so heated and the path can appear to be unmanageable and unbearable. But know that God cares about us and He sees what we can't. He sees every hot-spot, pothole, and resting place along our path. His arms are big enough to hold and cover us whenever necessary. Trust the process. Take shade when you need it, but keep pushing forward. I don't know how far you are into your walk, but be encouraged and know that your steps are ordered. We don't get sentenced to pain. Instead we are trusted to deal with the pain. The pain from the past cannot be allowed to interrupt present legacy. Dealing with pain during your process (whatever that is) is a part of establishing empathy, tenacity, and a genuine relationship with God.

The trouble you experience can either make you better or bitter. Look at your trials as opportunities to draw closer to God because doing so has the potential to open up doors in your life. The battles and afflictions you experience can be utilized for spiritual growth and a deepened knowledge of God and His Word. There are people attached to your growth, deliverance, and break through. Ask God for what you want and trust Him for what you need. His strength is perfect when our strength is gone. He'll carry us when we can't carry on. So cling to his help. Others might fail you but his help is consistent, holistic, and 100% available! And when you come through your refining process I hope to one day read your book or hear your story.

# The Help: Activity

How do you feel about asking for help?

What kind of help do you feel you need and what steps are necessary to get through what you're experiencing (prayer, talking, quality time, journaling, etc.…)

What inhibits you from reaching out for help?

If you could have all the support you need, what would that support look like?

# ~SELF-REFLECTION~

# PICTURE IT

# Support

# What Does Your Support Look Like?

There are a few questions you have to seriously ask yourself when addressing concerns about how support looks for you. Different people consider different actions, responses, and display of emotions as sufficient or adequate support. What you might consider basic or reasonable expectations, in the very same matter, could be considered unreasonable to someone else. For instance, I might believe that if I texted you and said, "I'm feeling sooo depressed and no one is ever available," that you should INSTANTLY text me back showing concern and asking me some good heart-felt questions about my situation. After all, I did just drop some serious hint words that expressed how much I didn't want to be ignored when I sent that message. But instead I might receive a text back in a few days, if at all, saying "it's going to be okay, pray about it." Whhhaaaaattt!?! No way! That has to be unacceptable! Who does that? Well…actually it happens quite often. So many things can happen to delay someone else's response and even how they respond [phone issues, family issues, fear, work, school, children, personal challenges, etc.…].

We don't wrestle against flesh and blood but against principalities, powers, rulers of darkness, and spiritual wickedness in high places (Ephesians 6:12). Can I let you in on a little secret? This might be hard to receive or even believe (I know it was for me), but we are not the only ones going through "life-changing" challenges. Yup! That was a bummer to find out! Coming from a rejected background and going through all the things I had experienced (sexual abuse, physical abuse, emotional abuse, neglect, manipulation, and identity confusion) sometimes heightened my awareness of how and when others responded to me. Your past experiences can sometimes affect your present expectations. The solution to that "issue" is not allowing how others react to affect how you respond. There has to come a point in life where you simply become free from people. Why? I'm glad you asked. You cannot control what other people do. You can only control how you receive it. It all starts in the mind. If you can figure out how to operate from a renewed mindset, you have the power to change your entire life experience.

God blessed me with so many thoughtful, wonderful, beautiful, and compassionate friends but there were times I dropped my head into my palm and thought, "Dude, what are you doing?" One day I was talking to one of my good friends about my life and how upset and sad I was feeling about some things. I told her I wanted to die and her response was kind of like... "Huh? That makes no sense. Why would you want to die?" I instantly shut down emotionally. I expected her response to be more like, "Oh my... What's going on? How can I help? Why don't you want to live?" Instead it was more like, "Get your life together girl." I know she meant well with her response. She would never intentionally hurt me but we were two different people with differing expectations and experiences. I couldn't expect her to know that her response was not what I was looking for. That's something I had to try and understand in my close relationships. That wasn't the only time she said something that kind of made me cringe a little, but she helped me understand that I have to communicate my experience, expectations, triggers, and sensitivities. When I started to communicate clearly she became more aware of where I was coming from and the use of her verbiage. I personally prefer that people just know what's going on in my head so that I don't have to explain it, but it doesn't quite work that way. It was a lesson learned and lesson applied!

I prayed and asked God to send me some consistent support and He showed out! My support came in so many different facets. God gave me a wonderful Bishop (Henry Fernandez of The Faith Center) to speak the Word into my life. He blessed me with different Minister's that prayed for and with me. He gave me a great worship leader, Philbert Lake, who speaks into my life all the time. God gave me several close friends that I can depend on for whatever I need. But one of the biggest things he gave me for support was my church! I attend a Mega Church in Florida that serves over 10,000+ members, yet I was able to connect with people and programs that helped me address life issues and build up my strength (physical, emotional, and spiritual). Through the church community I was able to participate in programs such as the School of Prophets (Henry Fernandez Institute), Daughters of Zion/ Woman of Destiny (Minister Darlene Hord), Discipleship Courses (The Faith Center), Spiritual Warfare Training (Pastor Ezekiel), Volunteer

Ministries, Music Ministry, Women Ministry, and so many other pertinent programs. I was able to gain strength while going through my process and connect to other people who were also going through their processes.

Whether you obtain support from your community, family, or church; it is vital that you become part of a support system. Don't face the world alone. There are people, programs, and communities created to help you address whatever it is you are experiencing. There is something for everyone. Whatever avenue you choose to help build your support, do so with an open heart and renewed thought process. Examine your thoughts, their origin, and how you plan to address them.

What has to happen, for you, in order to make you feel as though someone values who you are and cares about your situation? Think hard about this answer because whatever that answer is needs to be communicated to whomever you consider your support. I use to believe that there was a universal response to someone who was visibly hurting. But what I've come to learn is that what I expect from my support may not always line up with what a person can and will provide. Furthermore, just because our expectations don't line up doesn't mean that I am being rejected or mishandled. This was one of the hardest things for me to accept as a person struggling with suicidal thoughts. I couldn't understand why I wouldn't be considered a priority, even with my life in danger. It caused me to demonize others and blame them for being inconsiderate and insensitive. My experience or your experience can be very real and difficult to handle and it's okay to need "right now" attention and support. But what happens sometimes is that different people are dealing with different things and who you need may not always be available (emotionally, physically, spiritually, or intellectually) immediately. I only know ONE person that was able to be there for me 24/7! I could call on Him whenever, however, and wherever! His name is Jesus. He is as real as the light that shines each day. His presence has the power to shift your mindset. He cares for you so much. He took the time to form you and breathe life into your body. Whether you're a believer (of God) or not, He is still the same God yesterday, today, and forever more (Hebrews 13:8). I dare you to trust Him. I can say with 100% certainty that if you allow Him into your life, you'll never be the same.

Make a plan and stick to it!

**(Use this space to create a plan for something important to you)**

## <u>Support Plan</u>

**(Refer to this page whenever experiencing a crisis)**

Who do you contact for support?

Who would you like to contact for support?

What can you do to build your support system?

How do you know when you need to contact your support?

What are external (outside) factors that trigger feelings of sadness?

What internal (inside) factors trigger feelings of sadness?

What are some things that make you happy?

# Helpful Facts

**Recognizing Someone That Might Be Considering Suicide:**

1. Giving away personal items
2. Posting on social media about suicide, death, or finality with life
3. Change in appearance (unkempt)
4. Isolation from people
5. Excessive crying
6. Change in appetite
7. Decreased grades in school
8. Excessive weight loss or weight gain
9. Helplessness
10. Psychosis
11. Hopelessness
12. Intense emotional pain
13. Mood swings
14. Feeling trapped
15. Chronic illness

**Things You Should Avoid Saying to Suicidal Person:**

1. Just get over it.
2. There are other people going through more than what you are going through – although this could be true the individual is not at a place where they are thinking about another person's mishaps. Their focus is on what they are experiencing.
3. Just pray about it- Most of the time it takes physically doing something about the situation in addition to praying.
4. What's wrong with you? – How you verbalize what you're saying is important. This method of asking questions insinuates that the individual is flawed.
5. I can't help you. You need more professional help. – This could very well be true, but there are better ways of stating this. (Ex: How do you feel about seeking additional help? Maybe we can all work through some things together.)
6. Committing suicide is a coward's way out- name calling doesn't change the way a person experiences their situation.

**Questions You Can Ask:**

1. How can I help you? What are your needs?
2. How are you feeling?
3. What are you thinking or what's on your mind?
4. Have you made a plan to commit suicide?
5. Have you ever attempted to commit suicide in the past?
6. How's your relationship with God?
7. How would you like your relationship to be with God?
8. Is there anything I can do to help?
9. How's your relationship with your family?
10. Do you have a support system? If not, is there any particular support you are open to receiving?
11. What's a typical day like for you?
12. Have you been considering or participating in any activities that are high-risk?
13. How much rest are you getting?
14. Are you participating in any "numbing" behaviors?
15. Why don't you want to live?
16. If you could take a magic pill and everything was okay in your life, what would that look like?
17. Would you like to talk about what's going on?
18. What's your idea of a successful life and why?
19. How can I be a good friend to you at this time?
20. How can I pray for you?
21. Are you interested in obtaining professional help? Why or Why not?
22. What are some things you look forward to? (There needs to be a sense of hope)

**Helpful Tips**:

1. Be genuine.
2. Address feelings before addressing facts.
3. Pray and ask God to lead and direct your thoughts and what you say.
4. Listen- it's usually not about having answers. Sometimes a person just needs to be heard.
5. Directly respond to the person's needs.
6. Be mindful of who you get involved and how. Your actions can either improve or agitate the situation. Over reacting or under-responding can both negatively impact the situation.
7. A person can have suicidal thoughts, but not necessarily want to commit suicide.
8. Be aware of your body language (looking at watch or phone, leaning back, facial expressions) when communicating with a person you believe might be suicidal.
9. Give the individual a chance to express their hurts. It's their right and they probably haven't been allowed to express the things they need to anyone else.
10. Do not gossip!
11. Ask permission to physically touch the person- could have experienced extensive abuse and be uncomfortable with touch.
12. Pray before committing to any actions or conversation.
13. Remember that your actions tend to speak louder than whatever you can say.
14. There's power in connecting with additional people.
15. Exercise confidentiality.
16. If a person has plan to take their life, take what they say seriously and contact a professional or someone the individual trusts.
17. Set appropriate boundaries.

# <u>WANT TO REMAIN CONNECTED?</u>

Website: www.dawna-wright.com

Email: christianlifesurvival@gmail.com

## <u>Follow me on social media:</u>

Instagram: dawnawright

Periscope: dawnawright

Twitter: dawnawright

Facebook: dawna.wright1

{<u>Suicide Hotline</u>: 1-800-273-8255}

**Let's Stay Connected!**

**I want to hear your story!**

www.ingramcontent.com/pod-product-compliance
Lightning Source LLC
Chambersburg PA
CBHW072152020426
42334CB00018B/1975